AJ's Promise

AJ's Promise

Karla Erickson

Illustrations
by Sandy Gagon

Bookcraft
Salt Lake City, Utah

All characters in this book are fictitious,
and any resemblance to actual persons,
living or dead, is purely coincidental.

Library of Congress Catalog Card Number: 92-73808

ISBN 0-88494-849-8

First Printing, 1992

Printed in the United States of America

Contents

1

The Airport

"Our plane is late," said Mr. Bexton, as he returned from the ticket counter. "We've got about a forty-five minute wait until it leaves for Boston. We might as well relax." He picked up the evening paper from the chair beside him.

AJ sat quietly as her father started reading. She thought about her promise to Benj, her big brother who was on a mission in Germany. When Benj left the Missionary Training Center in Provo, he had challenged AJ to give away a Book of Mormon to a stranger. The day AJ knew she would be going on this trip with her father, she had written to Benj, promising to give one away to someone in Boston. She had also promised to write and tell him all about it. How she missed Benj! Two years away from him seemed almost unbearable. Maybe giving away the Book of Mormon would let her experience what it might feel like to be a missionary. That way, Benj would almost seem a little closer.

AJ reached to find her backpack, which held all her homework as well as a copy of the Book of Mormon.

"Dad," she asked, "have you seen my backpack? I can't find it."

"What backpack, AJ?" he asked, surprised. "I didn't notice it when I loaded the luggage into the car. And I didn't check it through with the suitcases."

"Dad! I think I left it on the couch in the family room. What will I do?" AJ felt her heart starting to pound fast. "I promised Miss Bleezer that I'd hand in all my work on Monday. She'll kill me if I don't have it done." AJ didn't want to mention her other reason for concern. Her promise to Benj was like a secret between the two of them. But she needed that Book of Mormon. Benj would be disappointed in her if she didn't give it away.

Her father laughed, not sensing AJ's anxiety. "Miss Bleezer won't *kill* you, AJ. Tell her you'll hand in your homework later."

"Dad, I can't do that. Isn't there any way we can make a quick trip home and get it?"

"We've got forty minutes," Dad answered, glancing at his watch. "I guess we could call Mom and ask her to bring it."

"Mom's at school with Sara," AJ said, her voice trembling.

"And of course, the older kids are in school, too," added her father.

"Dad, please—let's go home. I just can't go without my homework." By this time, AJ was close to tears.

"All right; don't get upset," her father said, folding the newspaper. "But to make sure we get on the flight, you stay here. When they start boarding, tell them I'm on my way."

With that, he grabbed his jacket and headed down the walkway. "Be sure to take my briefcase with you when you get on the plane," he called to AJ, as he started running toward the main terminal.

AJ looked around at all the people who had gathered at the ticket counter. Their flight must be full. She hoped the plane was as late as the attendant had indicated. She watched the second hand on the gigantic wall clock leisurely continue around the numbers. How is it that a minute can last so long? And yet it seems that hours pass so quickly.

AJ sat lost in thought about the passing minutes when she felt someone sit down next to her.

"Oops! Excuse me, Miss," said an elderly gentleman. "I just about sat right on your lap." He started to laugh at his own joke.

AJ smiled politely. She scooted over to give him more room.

"Are you going to Boston?" he asked.

"Yes, my father and I are both going," answered AJ. "But I forgot my school books. He went home to get them."

"You must live close around here," mused the man.

"Pretty close," answered AJ. "It takes about twenty minutes."

"Are you sure your dad can make it home and back? That's cutting it quite close," said the gentleman. His tone of voice had changed from joking to concern about AJ's plight.

AJ began to worry. What if her father had difficulty getting out of the parking lot? What if he had a flat tire on the way?

A loud voice came over the intercom. "Will all the passengers leaving for Boston prepare to board?"

AJ's heart raced. She couldn't board without her father. She just sat and fumbled with her ticket.

"C'mon, young lady," said the old man as he struggled to get out of the chair. "You'd better get on the plane."

"I'm going to wait for my father," replied AJ. "But thanks. Here, let me help you with your luggage."

The old gentleman smiled kindly, and with AJ's help he managed to make it to the counter with his carry-on luggage.

AJ went back to her seat. She was determined not to board without her father. *Those dumb old school books,* she thought. If Miss Bleezer wasn't such a horrible teacher, she wouldn't have given her all that homework. Then she wouldn't be in such a fix. She could have tucked the Book of Mormon in her purse, instead of worrying about a backpack.

One of the attendants motioned to AJ. "Are you Allison Judy Bexton, one of the passengers going to Boston?" she asked.

AJ nodded. She hated being called Allison Judy. Everyone called her AJ. But she realized her ticket must have had her name written out.

"It's time to board the plane," said the attendant.

"Could I wait for just a few more minutes?" AJ asked. "My father had to make a quick trip to our home, but he should be here any minute."

"We're now loading the last passengers. Why don't you board and we'll hold the plane as long as we can." The young attendant walked over to AJ and helped gather her belongings.

AJ stood by her chair, hesitating.

She didn't want to board. But she didn't have the courage to tell the attendant she wouldn't get on the plane.

AJ took out her ticket and tried to do everything as slowly as possible. She hoped every minute would get her father closer.

As she walked into the cabin of the plane, another flight attendant helped her find her seat. It was by the window. AJ eagerly looked out, trying to spot her father. She hugged his briefcase, trying to muster courage as she waited.

The minutes dragged on for what seemed like eternity. AJ jolted with fear when she heard the engines start. She felt the rumbling of the motor under her feet. Her heart pounded with fright. How could she ever go to Boston—alone!

She clutched the briefcase as the plane slowly started to back away from the boarding gate.

"Please! Please, Heavenly Father," she prayed silently. "Help Dad get on the plane."

The plane jerked to a stop. Slowly, it moved back to the loading gate. AJ's heart pounded and her stomach churned.

The flight attendant opened the door, and there

stood her father, grinning. AJ could not remember being so excited to see him. He was breathing hard and trying to catch his breath. His hair was a mess and his tie was partly undone. And slung around his shoulder was AJ's backpack.

"I bet you thought I'd miss the plane," he said, panting as he sat in the seat next to AJ.

AJ couldn't say a word. She was afraid she'd start crying. She just hugged her father tightly and silently thanked Heavenly Father.

"Thanks for getting my briefcase," her father said, as he tucked it under his seat.

"And thanks for getting my backpack," AJ said, grinning. At last she regained her composure. "Dad, I was really scared you might not make the plane. Did you know it had already left the gate?"

"Just as I ran to the ticket counter, I saw it moving away. I told them my daughter was on that plane and, somehow, I had to get on board."

"That must have been when they stopped the plane and drove back to the gate," said AJ. They both started laughing.

"I sure hope this isn't an indication of what the rest of our trip will be like," her father said.

"It isn't," said AJ confidently, snuggling close to him. At least, she hoped not.

2

The Hotel

As AJ unpacked her suitcase, she glanced out of the hotel window. "Dad," she called excitedly, "look at the huge tower! And there's a clock at the top."

She was fascinated by the numerous towering buildings. They seemed to stretch up as high as they could so they could catch their breath, apart from the smaller buildings that crowded around them.

"Tonight we'll go to dinner and then we can walk around the North End," said her father. "We can find out where the Freedom Trail begins."

"What's the Freedom Trail?" AJ asked.

"It's not exactly the kind of trail you're probably thinking of," her Dad answered. "When we go on a trail out in the West, we think of hiking into the mountains and following a worn path." He hung up his suits and then continued. "This trail is a trail of red paint, red bricks, and red footprints. It guides people to historic buildings and sites that are a part of American history. It's called the Freedom Trail because the people of Boston were fighting to free themselves from the British."

AJ walked over to another window. "There's a shopping center right over there, Dad," AJ announced. But it didn't look quite like the malls back home. There were small shops, and people were sitting outside under large umbrellas.

AJ's father walked over by the window. "That's not exactly a mall. It's called Faneuil Hall Marketplace or Quincy Market. But if you want to say it the way the Bostonians do, then you pronounce it like 'Quinzee Mahket.' They don't pronounce their r's. When they tell you to park your car, they say, 'Pahk youh cah.'"

AJ laughed. "Dad, they really don't talk like that, do they?"

"Some of them do," he said, as they headed out of the door. "Let's go to a wonderful little Italian restaurant in the North End. It has an atmosphere all its own. And then, on the way back, we'll walk through 'Quinzee Mahket.'"

AJ clutched her father's hand. They laughed at his attempt to speak Bostonian. Being alone with her father was more fun than she had imagined.

Once outside, she smelled the salty air, which seemed denser than the air back home. Their hotel was on the waterfront by Boston Harbor.

"There's a famous warship, the USS *Constitution* which was nicknamed 'Old Ironsides.' It's out in the harbor," her father told her. "On Saturday we'll go visit it and the museum. There's so much I want you to see."

As they strolled into the North End, AJ was fascinated by the cobblestone roads and by how narrow and tiny the streets were. "How could you ever drive our Suburban around here?" she asked.

Her father laughed. "I was once told to never try to drive a car in Boston. Instead, use the MBTA. It's their underground transit. We can probably walk to most of the places we want to see. But on Saturday, we'll ride the MBTA out to Fenway Park where the Boston Red Sox play."

"The Red Sox?" AJ's eyes sparkled. "Benj and I love that team."

AJ stared at the old buildings crowded together. She spotted an old wooden frame home with a sign which caught her attention. "Dad, this is Paul Revere's home!" she exclaimed. She enthusiastically read the inscription and informed her dad that it was the oldest structure in Boston, built in 1676. "I thought homes were old when they were twenty or thirty years old. This is really *old*," she said. "And Dad, here are some red bricks. This must be a part of the Freedom Trail."

"It sure is, AJ. But it looks like we're too late to go inside. Besides, my stomach's growling," her dad said. "Not too far from here is the Italian restaurant I told you about—Louie's."

For what was supposed to be a wonderful restaurant, Louie's was a lot different than AJ had imagined. It was just a small building, not fancy-looking at all. They were greeted by a dark-haired gentleman who motioned for them to follow him to a small, candlelit table. Actually, AJ thought, it was rather romantic. It reminded her of movies she had seen where people were sitting in dimly lit restaurants and the waiter was always a man carrying a white towel over his arm.

The waiter pulled back AJ's chair for her to sit down. What service!

Scanning the menu, AJ read a few familiar words like shrimp and oysters, but most of it seemed like another language.

"Why not try some fettuccine," her dad prompted. "Since this is an Italian restaurant, their pasta is excellent."

While they waited for their dinner, the waiter brought out warm bread and several choices of cheese. Delicious! AJ looked around at the other guests. There were no other children. And everyone was visiting quietly. She suddenly felt much older than twelve.

After a wonderful meal, they ventured out into the Italian neighborhood. AJ heard music. Many people had gathered right in the middle of the street. Someone was playing a hand accordion, and two people were dancing. As the crowd increased, the dancing couple started grabbing some of the spectators to dance with them. Before long, a raucous street dance was in full swing.

"Do they do this all the time?" asked AJ.

"Probably not *all* the time," answered her father. "Most likely, the guy with the accordion was playing his music when someone walking by thought it would be fun to dance."

AJ was fascinated. She had never seen anything like that in Salt Lake City. They continued down the street, looking in the miniature shop windows. What a magical world of tiny shops, hugging together to form a happy, noisy neighborhood!

"This is Faneuil Hall," Dad said, pointing to a large red building. "This is the same red hall you can see from our hotel, but we are now on the other side. Here are some more red bricks, which means that this is a part of the Freedom Trail."

"Dad," AJ said excitedly, "there's another crowd. Let's go see what's going on."

She grabbed his hand and pulled him toward a circle of people. Inside the circle was a young man atop a towering unicycle. He was dressed in a clown's suit, wearing a tall black top hat.

"He's really good, Dad. Does he do this every night?"

"Probably most nights, when the weather's nice. When he's through with his act, he'll put his hat on the ground and the spectators can drop money into it."

AJ reached into her pocket and fumbled for some quarters. When the cyclist finished his act and bowed to the cheering audience, AJ walked over and dropped four quarters into the black hat. Just as she turned to go back to her father, another street performer dressed in a black cape grabbed her by the arm.

"Would you like to help me in a magic act?" he asked.

AJ glanced at her father who was nearby. He grinned and nodded his approval. As the magician started some magic tricks a crowd gathered again, and AJ stood in the middle. He handed AJ a yellow hanky and told her to be careful with it because it was a very expensive hanky. So AJ clutched it tightly. The magician threw a white cloth over AJ's hand and when he reached under to pull out the yellow hanky, he pulled out a pigeon. AJ blinked with surprise.

"Where's my yellow, expensive hanky," the magician teasingly asked AJ. She shook her head.

"OK. I'll try again." This time he reached under the white cloth and pulled out a purple hanky, then a green, then a red. By this time the crowd was cheering, and AJ was as surprised as anyone.

The magician turned to AJ, and with a twinkle of merriment he said, "I bet you decided to keep my beautiful hanky and try to sell it for money. I must get it from you."

With that, he whipped off the white cloth and opened AJ's hand—only to find a green dollar bill. AJ had no idea where the yellow hanky had gone or how she had managed to get hold of a dollar bill.

The magician acted as if he were going to cry when he discovered no yellow hanky. He told AJ she could leave because she had not helped him. As AJ turned, the magician gently pulled the yellow hanky from the back of her jacket. The crowd cheered and the magician had AJ take a bow.

The tower clock struck ten o'clock. "I've got to get back to the hotel and have some sleep, AJ," her father said. "Tomorrow I have some important meetings. But in the afternoon, we'll find the beginning of the Freedom Trail. We can spend the afternoon sightseeing. And Saturday we'll go to the shipyard and museum and ride the MBTA to Fenway Park."

In the cool evening air, AJ snuggled close to her father. What a great time they had enjoyed already.

She imagined all the things they would see tomorrow. On the way to the hotel, they passed a smiling old lady holding a brown wicker basket. Inside it was a small, colorful bundle of fresh flowers. "Flowers?" she asked.

AJ's father smiled. He pulled out some change and bought the last bouquet. As he handed the flowers to AJ, the old lady grinned. "You have a pretty little lady there," she said.

"I sure do," AJ's father said, as he hugged AJ tightly. "I sure do."

3

Tim Hancey

"I hate to leave you and go to the office, AJ," said her father, straightening his tie. "I sure hope the meetings last only until one or two this afternoon. Do you have enough homework to last all that time?"

"I probably do," answered AJ, pulling out her books from her backpack. "I brought my library book along, too."

AJ's father was still concerned about leaving her in the hotel alone. "Let's go down into the lobby restaurant and catch a quick breakfast. That way I can talk to the desk clerk and ask her to help you if you need anything."

"Dad," AJ said, "don't be so worried about me. Really, I'm not afraid to stay here. And besides, I've got tons of homework."

"I would feel better if you at least met the desk clerk," said her dad. "Besides, you do need something to eat."

AJ could tell there was no use arguing. She hurried and dressed and brushed her long, dark hair into a ponytail. And her dad was right. She did need some breakfast.

Downstairs, her father introduced her to the desk clerk. "Mary, this is my daughter, AJ. She'll be staying in our room this morning while I go to a meeting. I sure would appreciate it if you'd keep an eye on her."

AJ was a little embarrassed. She was twelve years old. She didn't need someone keeping an eye on her. But she smiled politely. "Hello, Mary."

Mary smiled back. "No need to worry, Mr. Bexton. I'll be here all day."

After breakfast, as they walked back to the room, AJ quizzed her father. "Do you know Mary, Dad? She seemed to know you."

"Mary's from Utah. She's one of my partners' daughters. If she weren't working today, I'd probably make you go to the office with me," replied her dad. "But I feel a little better knowing she's here."

"Now, don't worry, Dad," said AJ. "If I leave the hotel for any reason, I'll be sure to tell Mary. Okay?"

"Okay," agreed her father. "I'll give you a call, around eleven, to let you know when I'll be back. Study hard," he said, as he made sure to lock the door. "And don't open the door for anyone except me, okay?"

AJ laughed. "Okay, Dad. Good luck with your meetings."

With her English homework, two assignments in math, and a lot of reading to do in social studies, AJ knew she'd have enough to keep her busy. She

15

switched on the television so the room wouldn't seem so quiet. But she didn't even notice what was on. She buried her thoughts in her homework.

AJ jumped when the phone rang. "AJ, this is Dad. We have a problem here in the office. Two more partners are coming in this afternoon, and I have to be here. How are you doing in the hotel?"

"I'm fine, Dad," AJ replied. "I'm almost done with my homework. How late do you think you'll be?"

"I don't know for sure. It looks like it could be as late as three or four in the afternoon. Would you be okay that long?"

"Sure," said AJ. "I'll just go down and grab a sandwich for lunch. I'll be sure to let Mary know where I am."

AJ hung up the phone, a little disappointed. She was getting hungry and she'd feel a lot better if her father were there to go to lunch with her.

AJ made sure she had her key as she locked the door to her room. She spotted Mary at the desk and walked over to tell her she was going to get a sandwich.

"Can you wait a few minutes, AJ?" asked Mary. "I get off for lunch in five minutes, and we could walk over to Quincy Market together."

AJ liked the suggestion. Now she wouldn't have to have lunch alone. Mary's enthusiastic and bubbly personality quickly won AJ's heart.

"Have you ever had one of Boston's huge pretzels covered with cheese?" she asked AJ.

AJ shook her head. Mary grabbed AJ's hand. "You are in for a real treat, AJ. The pretzels at Quincy Market are the best in Boston."

They hurried across the street. Mary knew just where to go. She took AJ to the pretzel place, then to a salad and yogurt shop. "Let's take our lunch outside and sit under an umbrella, AJ," Mary called as she looked for an empty table.

AJ agreed with Mary's judgment; she had never before tasted a pretzel which could compare to the cheese-covered one. Even the salad and yogurt seemed to taste extra good.

"Couldn't your father come to lunch?" Mary asked.

"Something came up at the office, and he said he might be a little late," answered AJ.

"Wish I didn't have to go to work this afternoon," said Mary. "We could take off and go see the sights. Have you ever been to Boston before?"

"No," answered AJ. "But last night Dad and I saw a few things, and I really do like it. He promised to take me on the Freedom Trail this afternoon."

"I love Boston," said Mary. "My oldest sister and her husband live here. When I first saw the place, I fell in love with it. That's why I decided to come here and work for a while. At first I thought I would be frightened. But the people here have been so good to me. I live with my sister, and her family belongs to an incredible ward. It's kinda like being out in the mission field. Oops! I guess I need to know if you are a Mormon, so you'd know what I'm talking about."

AJ grinned. "Yes, I'm a Mormon. And I have a brother, Benj, who is on a mission in Germany." AJ thought of her Book of Mormon in her backpack at the hotel room. "In fact, I promised Benj that I would give away a Book of Mormon to someone here in Boston."

Mary's eyes lit with interest. "AJ, that's a great idea. I bet you could find someone right here in Quincy Market to give it to."

Mary glanced at her watch. "Oh, no. I've been talking so much that my lunch hour is over. We'd better hurry back to the hotel."

Mary and AJ rushed across the street. "Thanks for a fun lunch, Mary," said AJ, as Mary hurried to put her hotel jacket on.

"That was fun, AJ," said Mary. "Maybe we can do something later, during my afternoon break."

Suddenly the lobby was filled with a tourist group from the Midwest. AJ went back to her room. She kept thinking about her conversation with Mary. Could she really find someone in Quincy Market to give her Book of Mormon to? She gazed out her window toward the market. Mary didn't seem afraid to be alone in Boston. Why should she? AJ grabbed the Book of Mormon. "Here I go, Benj," AJ said aloud as she locked the hotel room. Excitement surged through her body. She felt like a missionary, heading out for an unknown land to share the gospel.

Mary was at her desk and swamped with people, all wanting her attention. AJ motioned to her that she was going back to Quincy Market. Mary waved. "I'll let you know when I get back," AJ called, hoping Mary had heard.

The sunshine was warm and AJ's heart was beating with excitement as she tucked the Book of

Mormon under her arm. She looked at an older man sitting alone at a table, and she spied a young couple at another table. How did missionaries go up to people and start talking? she wondered. She walked up and down Quincy Market and eyed all of her prospective contacts. Her enthusiasm was slowly dying. How do I start a conversation? she wondered.

Dejectedly, AJ walked over to the yogurt shop where Mary had taken her. Next door was a sweet shop, and AJ decided some candy might taste good. Just as she reached into her pocket, she felt a hard thud against her shoulder, and suddenly she was lying sprawled on the ground.

"Uh, sorry about that," said a voice behind AJ. "I really didn't mean to knock you down."

AJ felt a helpful hand reaching under her arm to lift her up. A young boy, a little older than she, was standing there looking at her. He had dark, curly hair and dark—almost black—eyes.

"Guess I wasn't watching where I was going," he apolo- 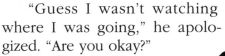 gized. "Are you okay?"

"Sure, I'm all right," AJ said, still feeling surprised.

"I know—to show you that I'm sorry, I'll even buy you a candy bar," said the stranger.

He reached into his pocket for change. "Which one would you like?"

"You don't have to buy me any candy. Really, I'm okay," said AJ.

The boy looked at AJ as if he were studying her. "You must be a visitor. Right?" he asked.

"I'm here with my father," replied AJ. "I live in Salt Lake City."

"Salt Lake City . . . um. Isn't that somewhere out in the West?" he asked.

AJ was stunned. What an idiot! He didn't even know where Salt Lake City was. "Actually, it's in the state of Utah. Do you know where that is?" AJ asked, a little sarcastically.

But instead of being embarrassed, the boy just cocked his head and said, "I told you it was in the West. By the way, my name is Tim. Tim Hancey. What's yours?"

"AJ."

Tim started laughing. "Now you're probably going to ask me if I know what AJ stands for. Is it for a name out West, too?"

Tim laughed and must have thought what he said was pretty funny. But AJ just stood there and looked at him. She didn't think he was funny at all. In fact, he was quite cocky and much too sure of himself. She turned to leave.

"Hey, don't forget your book here on the ground," said Tim as he picked it up and handed it to AJ.

AJ reached for the book as Tim read the title. "Book of Mormon," he said. "What kind of book is it?"

AJ froze. She didn't know what to say. "It's just a book of mine," she finally answered. Her conscience jabbed her. Missionaries wouldn't be hesitant to tell someone about the Book of Mormon. Why should she be? Quickly AJ added, "It's a book which tells about Jesus Christ." AJ couldn't believe that she had said that.

Tim's eyebrows deepened into a frown. "You mean you go around with church books?"

"It's a book my church believes in," said AJ. She felt so stupid. Everything she said sounded stupid. "My big brother went on a mission for our church. I promised that I would give away a Book of Mormon."

Now she knew that Tim was totally confused, and she felt her cheeks flushing. Why had she ever gone to the candy shop?

A big grin crossed Tim's face. "I don't understand anything you're telling me," he said. "Why don't we go sit down and you can explain what you're talking about."

They found an empty table and AJ started again. "I'm a Mormon from Utah. Do you know what Mormons are?" she asked Tim.

Tim shook his head, so AJ continued.

"Actually, my church is called The Church of Jesus Christ of Latter-day Saints. We have these scriptures, called the Book of Mormon. In our church, when guys are nineteen years old, they can go on a mission for two years to tell people about the Church. My big brother, Benj, was called to serve in Germany and he will be there for two years, telling the German people about the gospel."

Tim acted a little interested. "When did your brother learn to speak German?" he asked.

"Well, he studied it for two months before he left for Germany," AJ replied. She still felt that everything she was saying was not making any sense to Tim.

Tim's black eyes lit with sarcasm. "You mean that your big brother let someone send him to Germany just so he could talk about religion? I'll bet he took the money and is having a great time over there." Tim laughed.

AJ didn't think he was one bit funny. "He didn't take anyone's money. He saved his own money and he's using that. And he's not over there having a party, either. He's over there telling people about the Church."

"Wow! He must be some religious geek to do that," said Tim. "I never have liked religion. It just seems that everyone who is religious is a hypocrite and afraid to stand on his own two feet."

AJ was furious. "Benj is no geek and for sure not a hypocrite," she blurted. "And he's not afraid of anything. I wish he were here right now to talk to you. Maybe he could put some sense into your stupid head." AJ couldn't believe that Tim could make her so angry. She shouldn't have reacted so strongly.

Tim just laughed. "You sound like my Grandma Hancey. In fact, you two would get along just great. Grandma's always talking to me about religion. But no one's going to get me hooked into that. I've never needed any religion and I get along just fine."

"How can you say that, Tim?" AJ asked incredulously. "Aren't there some times when you really need extra help and you want to ask for it?"

Tim looked a little more serious. "Oh, yeah, there was a time when I needed help. But instead of help, I just got ignored."

AJ sensed that Tim was holding some deep, hurt feelings inside. She really didn't like his haughty nature, but for some reason she was drawn to him. "Did you once believe?" she asked.

"Believe? Believe in what? You don't believe in something that does nothing for you. I don't know how my grandmother keeps believing. She was just as hurt as I was."

AJ relaxed her defensive accusations. "How were you hurt, Tim?"

Tim suddenly regained his arrogance. "Hey, let's not waste a great day like this talking about religion. If you've got some time, why don't you come and meet my grandmother. She would really like you. You two could talk about religion all afternoon." Tim laughed sarcastically.

"No, I can't," said AJ. "My dad's at a meeting, and I have to be at the hotel when he comes back." AJ got an idea. "But you can do me a great favor." She handed the Book of Mormon to Tim. "I sure would like you to give this book to your grandma."

"No way," said Tim. "If you want her to have that book, then you have to give it to her herself."

Tim started to walk away.

"I can't," said AJ. "I've got to stay here. Besides, I don't know Boston and I'd get lost trying to get back to the hotel."

Tim turned around to face her. "Look, I don't live very far away. Can't you leave a note for your dad?"

"I can tell the desk clerk where I'm going," said AJ. "Do you want to come over to the hotel with me?"

Tim shrugged his shoulders. "Might as well."

AJ was glad the tourists were not around the desk when they entered the lobby. "Hi, Mary," said AJ. "If Dad calls for me, can you tell him I'm at Quincy Market?"

Mary glanced at Tim standing next to AJ. "And who should I say you are with at Quincy Market?" she teased.

"Oh, this is Tim Hancey. He lives close by, and we might go meet his grandmother," said AJ.

"Hancey. Is your grandmother Adelaide Hancey?" Mary asked Tim.

Tim almost looked embarrassed. "Yes. Do you know her?"

"I sure do," said Mary. "She is one of my favorite people. So you're her grandson who lives with her? She's told me a lot about you."

"Then do you think it would be okay if Tim takes me to meet her?" asked AJ. She felt much better knowing that Mary knew the Hanceys and liked them.

"Just be sure to have Tim bring you back here, so you don't get lost. Is that a promise?" asked Mary. "I don't want to get in trouble with your father."

AJ clutched the Book of Mormon as she and Tim left the hotel. If Mary knew Grandmother Hancey so well, why hadn't Mary told her and Tim about the Church?

The autumn day was warm and sunny. AJ loved the smell of the ocean water. She loved the crowded marketplace. She loved the quaint buildings and the feeling that she was a part of a city which had a strong foothold in American history. She loved Boston.

4

Grandmother Hancey

"C'mon this way," Tim said, as he pointed in the direction of Faneuil Hall and Quincy Market. "We live over in the North End, which is close to Paul Revere's house."

AJ walked fast to keep up with Tim. "That's where my dad took me last night to dinner. We walked past Paul Revere's house. But we couldn't go in because it was too late. Do you think we could stop and go inside?" asked AJ.

"Probably," replied Tim. "It costs a little bit, but not much." He grinned as he noticed how excited AJ was to see the old historical place.

AJ spotted some red bricks as part of the sidewalk. "We must be getting close, because we're on the Freedom Trail."

"Hey, who's the guide? You or me?" Tim asked teasingly.

As they rounded the corner, there stood the

quaint, historic house. It was an old frame building, marked by an American flag hanging from the second story. AJ and Tim paid for tickets and they walked inside. They walked into the Best Chamber, which was really the master bedroom suite. AJ was intrigued with the poster bed and the time-worn furniture. On a small desk by the bed was a table with a jar and a feather-plume pen. Candles also adorned the table.

AJ tried to imagine life in a home like this. She would have happily stayed for a long time to examine every little detail, but Tim was growing uneasy.

"If we're going to get back in just a couple of hours, we'd better get on our way," Tim said to AJ. "I can see you like this kind of stuff, but you can have your dad bring you back tomorrow."

Tim had seen it all so many times that it had lost some of its attraction. AJ, on the other hand, was caught up in the fact that Paul Revere had actually lived in that house with his wife, mother, and eleven children. Paul Revere had always been just another name in American history to her, until now. AJ's eyes were filled with excitement.

"I can't believe you live so close to places like this, Tim," she said. "If I lived here, I'd go sightseeing every day."

Tim just laughed at her. "Maybe you would for a week or so. But after a while they'd become just everyday, common things to you. Do you still get excited about the history in your state of Utah?"

AJ had to admit that Tim was probably right. There were things about Utah which she took for granted, things that Tim would probably find quite interesting. "I guess I do act pretty dumb about these places," AJ said. "But I do like it here. And I like to see these places that I've read about in history."

As they left the building, a black car turned suddenly into the tiny, narrow street near them. Four men, dressed very nicely in dark suits, climbed out of the car. AJ couldn't help but notice them. And Tim took notice, also.

"Those are probably Mafia men," he said casually to AJ, knowing he would get her attention.

AJ looked somewhat apprehensive. "What exactly is the Mafia?" she asked.

Tim grinned at his chance to frighten AJ. "Many years ago the Mafia was formed in Italy. It's kinda like a secret gang. Haven't you ever read about Al Capone and some of those guys? How they'd go around killing people who got in their way?"

AJ shook her head as she walked closer to Tim.

"Well," Tim continued, "the North End of Boston is Italian. You can always tell someone who belongs to the Mafia because they wear dark suits and shiny, black shoes."

"Doesn't it scare you to live around them?" asked AJ.

Tim knew his plan had succeeded. AJ was walking right next to him and keeping up with his fast pace. He grinned. "Nope. You just go around doing your own business and you don't have to worry. Just don't ever let anyone know you're afraid, and you'll be okay."

AJ took a deep breath. She'd be glad when they reached Grandmother Hancey's. She'd suddenly lost her desire to see more landmarks.

AJ could no longer tell where they were. They were off the Freedom Trail and she had lost sight of the street of Paul Revere's house. She was really thankful that she had Tim to take her back to the hotel.

They turned into another narrow street and Tim took hold of AJ's arm and pointed to some stairs leading into a basement room. He motioned for her to go down them. AJ took hold of a black handrail and went down about six steps. Wrought iron bars were on the two basement windows. Tim opened the door and walked inside.

"Hi, Grandma," he called out. "I'm home."

A white-haired, smiling lady came out from one of the back rooms. She was only about five feet high, by AJ's guess. Her eyes were deep brown and her skin was a pretty olive color. She seemed surprised to see them.

"What are you doing out of school, Tim?" she asked. But before he could answer, she caught sight of AJ and added, "And who is this pretty friend of yours?"

"This is AJ, Grandma," answered Tim. He skipped saying why he was out of school. "She's visiting from Utah and I met her at Faneuil Hall."

"Utah. That's where they have the big, salty lake, isn't it?" Grandmother replied. "Nice to meet you, AJ. How long are you staying?"

AJ was glad that Tim's grandmother knew about Utah. "Only this weekend," AJ replied. "My father had business in Boston, so he asked me to go with him. Right now, he's at meetings and I have to go back pretty soon and meet him."

Tim had been right. From the first moment AJ laid eyes on his grandmother, she liked her. She fidgeted with the Book of Mormon. She had no idea how she was going to give it away.

"Did you say you met AJ at Faneuil Hall?" asked Grandmother. "What were you doing there?" She looked straight at Tim for an answer this time.

Tim just laughed. "Grandmother, don't get upset. My history class had a field trip to Faneuil Hall to talk about how it was the 'Cradle of Liberty.' I've been there so many times and heard the story just as often. I figured no one would miss me. So I just slipped away to get something to eat. That's where I met AJ. I knocked her over," he said and started to laugh.

"Tim Hancey. That's no laughing matter. Now I'll have to call the school and make sure everything is okay. And that was pretty rude to knock AJ down."

AJ interrupted. "It was just an accident. Really."

Tim continued. "AJ has something she wants to give you, Grandma."

AJ's stomach started churning with apprehension. "I'm a Mormon from Utah, and in my church we have scriptures which tell more about Jesus Christ. I promised my brother, Benj, who is a missionary in Germany for our church, that I would give this book to someone in Boston. Tim said maybe you would want it." AJ handed the book to Grandmother.

To AJ's surprise, tears filled Grandmother's eyes. What had she said wrong?

Grandmother took hold of the book, and with teary eyes looked at AJ. "I have a very dear friend. She's young and beautiful and she's from Utah, too. She has told me about this church of yours. She also told me about a wonderful book which I must read someday. This must be the book she was talking about."

"Is your friend's name Mary, Grandmother?" Tim asked. "We met someone who works at the hotel where AJ is staying, and she said she knows you."

Again, Grandmother's eyes spilled with tears. "So you met Mary. Forgive me for being so sentimental and all. But everything Mary has told me about her church is just what I've been looking for all my life. She promised to take me to church with her this weekend. My, she will be surprised when I show her this book you gave me."

Tim grunted. "Grandma, you always get so worked up over religion. I don't know how you can believe in God when he has never answered your prayers or helped you."

"Tim Hancey," Grandmother said a little sternly. "How do you know that God has never answered my prayers? I'm always telling you how thankful we should be for his many blessings to us."

AJ stood quietly listening. She didn't say anything because this seemed like a much-too-private conversation.

Tim's eyes glared with anger. "If God answered your prayers, then why did he let Mom and Dad die in the car crash? We were all alive when the police arrived. Why did *they* have to die? Why was I the only one left to live? While they were at the hospital, I remember your praying that they would make it. And even I believed they would. I believed because you believed. And they both died. How can you say your prayers have been answered?"

AJ took a deep breath. She now understood the deep hurt feelings which she had sensed earlier from Tim.

Grandmother walked over to Tim. "I have *you*, Tim. And you've been one of my greatest blessings. I still don't understand why your parents died. But I know that God knows the answer. And I'm content that he let me keep you."

Tim just pulled away from his grandmother. But she continued, "Someday, Tim, I know you'll have a need to call upon someone for help."

"Never!" shouted Tim. "I know how to get along by myself. I don't need anyone. And for sure I don't need to pray." He left the room, and Grandmother and AJ stood facing each other.

"I'm so sorry this had to happen," Grandmother said. "Please don't hold anything against Tim. He's a good boy and has so many good things about him. I just know that God will look over him and help him find someone who can soften his heart."

AJ smiled. "That's okay. I'm just glad you're excited about your Book of Mormon. I've been reading it myself. Sometimes I don't understand all it says, but my family reads it; and my parents tell me all the time that it has answers to every problem I will ever have in life."

"You sound just like Mary," Grandmother said. "I love to hear her talk about your church. She said there are some missionaries here in Boston who would like to come and meet me. I must invite them over. But for right now, let's have a bite to eat. I imagine you and Tim are a little hungry."

As Grandmother and AJ walked into the miniature kitchen, Tim came out from the back room. He had apparently cooled down and was back to his happy, teasing self. He watched AJ help his grandmother cut up some cheese.

"I told AJ that you two would get along just great," he said.

Grandmother had so many questions for AJ. "What is your family like?" she asked. "How is it your father has business out here in Boston?"

AJ's mind flashed back to her family. "You'd like them. First, my dad has clients out here in Boston and that's why he had to fly here. I have two sisters. The oldest is Jennifer and she's a cheerleader. Then I have a little sister, Sara, who is only in first grade, and she's really cute."

AJ felt almost homesick as she talked about her family.

"Then I have twin brothers, Jacob and Josh. They're in high school and they're really good in sports. My mom is wonderful. She doesn't have a job other than taking care of all of us, and she does a lot of work in the church and at our schools."

"My, my," said Grandmother. "You do have quite the family. And what about that brother who is in Germany?"

"That's Benj. He's the oldest of our family and he went to Germany on a mission for two years. The reason I brought a Book of Mormon with me was because I promised him I'd give one away."

"And I'm so glad I'm the lucky person. I'll have to write that brother of yours and tell him how I like it. Would you like me to do that, AJ?" asked Grandmother.

AJ was excited about Grandmother's idea. Benj would be so proud of her. She couldn't believe everything was turning out so well. She loved being a missionary.

Grandmother Hancey's apartment was small compared to AJ's home. There were only two tiny bedrooms boxed between a bathroom, the small living room, and the miniature kitchen. But AJ felt comfortable and cozy. She sensed a wonderful spirit. As they ate lunch, Grandmother told AJ about some of the sights she must see while in Boston.

As Grandmother talked, her eyes sparkled with enthusiasm for the fascinating city. Even Tim joined in with suggestions on what to see. "Don't forget Fenway Park. Someday maybe you can come and see a Red Sox game."

The mention of Fenway Park brought AJ back to the present. "I'd better get going," she said as she glanced at her watch. "Dad said he might be out of his meetings at three or four, and it's nearly three o'clock right now. Tim, can you still take me back to the hotel?"

Just as AJ suggested that she must leave, Grandmother started gasping for her breath. Tim rushed to her side. "Grandmother! Grandmother! What's wrong?"

AJ's heart filled with panic as she watched Grandmother tumble onto the floor.

5

The 911 Number

Tim and AJ rushed to Grandmother's side. She could hardly speak to them. "I feel . . . terribly sick, Tim," she whispered. "I had . . . a sharp pain in my left arm. Uh . . . I can . . . hardly breathe. Please . . . just help me . . . get to my bed."

AJ and Tim lifted Grandmother to the bed and covered her with a light quilt. She looked deathly pale.

"Tim, we've got to get some help," said AJ. "Something's terribly wrong with your grandmother."

Tim sat by his grandmother, watching her rub her arm. "Just don't panic, AJ," he said. "Grandmother will tell us what to do."

"Maybe she doesn't know what to do," said AJ. "I think we'd better call for help."

Tim glared at her. She didn't know if he wanted her to be quiet or to get out of the room. "Grandmother will be okay. She just fainted."

Grandmother reached for Tim's arm. "Do something . . .Tim," Grandmother whispered. "My chest . . . is tight. . . I can hardly . . . breathe. Get help."

"Who do I go for?" he asked. "Do you want me to get a doctor?"

Grandmother could hardly say anything. She was losing ground quickly, and AJ knew something had to be done fast. "I'm calling 911 for help," she said, rushing to the phone. "Maybe *you* don't think we need them, Tim, but I do. Your grandmother is really sick."

AJ dialed 911. She couldn't believe how much in control she was. Tim stayed by his grandmother's side.

"What's your address?" AJ asked him. "I need to tell them where to send the ambulance."

Tim recited an address, and AJ confidently and efficiently repeated it over the phone. She looked over at Grandmother, whose eyes were closed. Tim was frozen with fear.

"Tim," AJ said, nudging him to reality, "go outside and watch for the ambulance so you can show them where to come. I'll stay here with Grandmother."

Tim ran up the stairs and AJ took Grandmother's hand in hers. "Dear Heavenly Father," she prayed. "Please watch over Grandmother Hancey. Tim and I don't quite know what to do. But help us do what we need to do for her. Please, don't let her die."

AJ felt tears running down her cheeks. She had only met Grandmother Hancey a few hours ago. But in that short time she had grown very fond of her.

Tim needed her. He couldn't have his grandmother die, too. He would never believe that God loved him.

AJ rubbed Grandmother's hand lightly. Grandmother's breathing was erratic and she was still very pale. AJ wished her father were there; he'd know what to do—as he did the time Jake was hurt when they were all snowmobiling. He looked like he was dead, lying under the huge machine. Dad blessed him, and AJ knew she'd never forget the calmness and peace that came over her. If only he could be there now to bless Grandmother!

The blaring ambulance interrupted AJ's thoughts. Two paramedics, dressed in green uniforms, rushed into Grandmother's room. They had all kinds of paraphernalia which they were strapping around Grandmother. They must be taking her vital signs, thought AJ. They worked quickly and talked between themselves quietly, so AJ couldn't tell what they were saying.

Tim struggled to get close to his grandmother. "Is she going to be all right?" he asked the paramedic.

"Don't know, son," he replied. "She's apparently had a massive heart attack, and it will just depend on how fast we can get her to an emergency room."

They quickly laid Grandmother on a stretcher and very carefully carried her up the tiny stairwell. Tim's face was gaunt as he turned to AJ. "This is all the help Grandma gets for believing," he said angrily. "All of this talk about your religion sure hasn't helped her, has it?"

AJ stood stunned. In just a few minutes her happiness at meeting Grandmother and telling her about the gospel and about her family had suddenly erupted into a horrible scene. Tim ran over to the medic who was putting Grandmother into the ambulance. Two police cars had arrived and their lights were flashing. Passersby stopped to see what was happening.

The policemen tried to disperse the crowd so the ambulance could leave. AJ was shoved back into the crowd. She couldn't see what they were doing to Grandmother. Her heart raced. Where was Tim?

She jumped up the side of the stair railing in time to see Tim motion to the medic. "That's my grandmother; I'm coming with you," he yelled to the paramedic. Just as the paramedic was ready to close the ambulance door, Tim jumped inside. The police kept pushing the people back, and then they got into their cars and turned on their sirens. The crowd quickly made way for the ambulance and police cars. With lights flashing and sirens blaring, the police and ambulance sped away.

"Where are they taking the old lady?" a passerby asked.

"I think they said she had a heart attack and they were taking her to the hospital," replied another.

The crowd slowly broke up. AJ was still holding on to the railing. Everything had happened so quickly that she could hardly believe it. She was worried about Grandmother. How she hoped they would get her to the hospital in time! How would she ever know?

Mary. She'd ask Mary to let her know. She had to hurry and find Mary and tell her what had happened.

AJ looked around at Grandmother's neighborhood. When Tim had brought her there, it looked so friendly and inviting. Suddenly, it all looked so frightening. She felt all alone. She took a deep breath and tried to determine which way they had come from. If she could just remember the way back to Paul Revere's house, she knew she could get back to the hotel.

If only the police were still there. She could ask them to take her back to the hotel. But the streets were barren, except for an old bent-over man who shuffled towards her. AJ was terrified.

"Are you lost, little girl?" he asked in a gruff voice. "If you've got some money, maybe I can help you." He came closer to AJ.

"N-no," AJ stammered. "I'm not lost. I'm just waiting for my grandmother to come."

"Don't you have some money for an old man?" he asked her, in a shaky voice. His bearded face was grimy; his teeth were yellow and some were missing. His clothes were tattered and he smelled awful.

AJ fumbled in her pocket and found some change. "Here," she muttered, dropping the money into his hand. "Now, please leave me alone."

She thought she heard the old man laugh. But she stood straight and acted as though she really was waiting for someone.

When the old man had disappeared from sight AJ tried to collect her senses. She had to find her way out of the neighborhood. The corner store looked a little familiar and she decided to walk in that direction.

Just then a black, shiny car drove by. It reminded her of the one she and Tim had seen on their way to Grandmother's. She kept thinking of what Tim had told her about the Mafia. She quickened her step and slipped into the grocery store at the corner. She peered out of the window to make sure the black car didn't stop. She couldn't see it anywhere.

I know what I'll do, AJ thought. *I'll just find a phone and call the hotel.* She hastily reached into her pocket. Nothing. She had given everything to that old beggar. Her face felt flushed and her heart pounded.

Get hold of yourself, AJ told herself. AJ walked out of the store and decided to walk in the direction from which she thought she and Tim had come. With her head held high, and trying to act as if she knew where she were going, she started walking.

Now remember that Walgreen store, she told herself. *And remember that barber shop.* If she could just see something which looked familiar, she would be okay.

Why didn't I notice where we were going? she scolded herself.

AJ looked at her watch. Three-thirty. Her father might be coming back from his meetings. AJ hoped he would be a little late so she could make it back to the hotel ahead of him. Her father would be terribly worried if she weren't there.

AJ kept walking, noticing the different stores

and making note of where each one was. She thought she recognized a pastry shop and was delighted.

It'll be no time at all until I'm back at the hotel, she told herself reassuringly. Just remember what Tim said: Always act as if you know what you're doing and where you're going. No one will bother you, then.

AJ turned a corner and was ecstatic. She recognized the store. *Was that the one Tim and I saw? Or . . .* Her heart froze. That was the Walgreen store near the street where Grandmother lived. No! AJ panicked. Her fears were confirmed. She saw the stair railing and the bars on the windows of the apartment. Without realizing it, she had been walking in circles. She was back at Grandmother Hancey's apartment.

AJ's heart raced. How could it be? She had been so careful to look at all the stores. She had taken note of where she was walking. What would she do now? Fear gripped her, as she had to admit she was lost . . . lost in Boston!

6

The Mafia

AJ heard shuffling footsteps behind her and she swung around. "No need to be scared, little girl," said a stringy, raspy voice. "It's only Grelda."

AJ couldn't believe her eyes. Standing before her was a tattered old woman carrying a brown bag with handles.

"It's just old Grelda, dear," she repeated again. "Come with Grelda, and you can help Grelda find something to eat."

AJ didn't know what to do. She was frightened of the old woman, yet she was also curious about her. Why was she carrying that old brown bag? What did she mean that AJ could come with her and help her find food?

Much too soon, AJ's questions were answered. She watched the old woman reach into the garbage cans standing by the side of the street. Grelda carefully sorted through the bags of garbage. AJ could not believe her eyes.

"Oh, lookie here, little girl," she called to AJ. "Grelda will eat good tonight. Yes, sir. Here's a sandwich for old Grelda."

"Oh, no," called AJ. "Don't eat that. It's dirty. It'll make you sick."

The old woman backed away from AJ and hid the sandwich behind her back. "Don't try and take this away from Grelda, or Grelda will get very mad," said the old woman. Her eyes glared, showing her intent on keeping the sandwich for herself.

"I won't take it away from you," AJ said. "I just don't want you to get sick."

The old woman laughed. "You promise not to take Grelda's sandwich? Okay. You can walk with me."

"Where is your home?" AJ asked. "Do you live around here?"

AJ hoped the woman did live nearby so she could ask for directions. But AJ was not prepared for Grelda's answer.

"Grelda lives here," she said, holding her arm out and pointing all around her.

"Do you mean you live on the streets?" asked AJ.

"Grelda lives here." And again she held out her arm and pointed all around her.

AJ's fear of being lost was temporarily blotted out of her mind. Grelda commanded her absolute attention.

"Grelda needs to rest," she said, as she shuffled towards a bench. She motioned for AJ to follow her. AJ watched as Grelda hungrily ate the half-eaten sandwich.

"Mmm. This is good," she said, with her mouth full. "Grelda has nice meal today."

AJ had read accounts about street people. She and her family had helped homeless people in her own town. But to meet a real, live bag lady was something she hadn't planned on.

"Is Grelda's little girl hungry?" she asked, holding up a crust of the sandwich for AJ.

Grelda's little girl? AJ mused, and then smiled warmly at the old woman. "No, I'm not hungry. But thank you for being so kind."

AJ felt the old woman's hand on her knee. "Grelda's little girl needs to eat, too."

AJ put her hand on top of the old woman's and patted it. "No, I'm okay," she said.

AJ looked into Grelda's deep blue eyes. She must have quite the story to tell, thought AJ. She noticed how dirty and worn Grelda's clothes were. Her face was lined with many years of living—or perhaps with few years of living a very hard life. Grelda looked almost frightening, but her eyes shone with kindness and they modified her grubby and tattered appearance.

When AJ patted Grelda's hand, she felt the old woman move closer to her. "Where is Grelda's little girl going?" she asked.

Immediately, AJ remembered her plight. "I'm trying to find my way back to my hotel," she said, trusting that the old lady would help her.

"Grelda will show you where to go," she said. "Just walk with Grelda."

"But you didn't ask where I needed to go," said AJ, confused.

"No matter," said the old woman. "Just come with Grelda."

No way, thought AJ. *I got into this mess by going with Tim to an area I didn't know. I can't do that again.*

"I have to get back to my hotel," AJ told her. "Can you show me how to get to Paul Revere's house?"

"Yes, yes, just come with Grelda," she said, as she motioned for AJ to follow her. Reluctantly, AJ followed. They walked along the same street AJ had already circled once. She recognized the different stores and knew that at least she wasn't too far from Grandmother Hancey's apartment.

"Taffy! Taffy!" the old woman called.

Who on earth is Taffy? wondered AJ.

Presently a scruffy, mangy, yellow dog sidled up to Grelda's side.

"Here's Grelda's Taffy," she said excitedly. "Taffy, here is Grelda's new little girl." She pointed over at AJ.

So Taffy was the dog. He sure wasn't much to look at. But Grelda acted as though he were the most beautiful dog in the world.

"Come get your lunch from Grelda," she said lovingly to the mangy animal. Taffy sniffed the brown paper bag as Grelda handed him the remains of the crusts off the sandwich she had found in the garbage.

AJ glanced at her watch. It was after four, and she knew her father must be out of his meetings. She must find her way to the hotel.

"Grelda, can you help me get to Paul Revere's house?" she pleaded. "I just need you to show me where to go."

Grelda smiled, but AJ knew that nothing she

had said even registered with Grelda. She just sat smiling at the old mangy dog and patting him on the head.

"I have to go, Grelda. Really," said AJ. "Thank you for being so kind to me. Take good care of Taffy."

Grelda smiled again. Her blue eyes still radiated love; yet AJ sensed that Grelda was in a world all her own. Without even thinking, she bent over and hugged the old woman and gave her a quick kiss on her cheek.

"'Bye, Grelda," said AJ. Her heart tugged as the old woman's eyes filled with tears.

"'Bye, little girl," she said.

As AJ walked away, she glanced back to see the old woman still patting Taffy's head.

Grelda could be someone's grandmother, AJ thought. She could be like my grandmother . . . or Tim's. AJ thought of her grandmother back in Utah. She, too, had a dog. Only, Miranda was a beautiful, clean, golden retriever.

I don't understand this world, mused AJ. *Why is it that we all belong to Heavenly Father, and yet some are like Grelda and Taffy and others are like Grandmother and Miranda? Does Heavenly Father favor some more than others?*

A car horn honked. It was a taxi, and the driver was yelling at AJ to watch where she was going. AJ quickly jumped back onto the curb. She dismissed the thoughts of Grelda and Taffy. She had to get back to the hotel. It was late. Her dad would be worried. And *she* was worried about Grandmother Hancey.

She took a deep breath and decided to try once more. *I must find Paul Revere's house,* she told herself. She started walking faster.

As she looked around at the buildings, she couldn't recognize one of them. At least she wasn't walking in circles. She kept walking faster and faster. But she had a strange feeling that she was going in the wrong direction. Frantically, she turned and headed the other way, walking faster than ever.

Out of breath, AJ slowed down. Tears filled her eyes. She was lost. Dead lost. She needed help. Surveying the buildings quickly, she spotted an alleyway. Walking over to it, she looked up both sides of the street to make sure she was alone. She leaned against the brick wall, bowed her head and, with tears streaming down her cheeks, she quietly said: "Dear Heavenly Father, I'm lost. I don't know what to do. I need your help. Please help me find my way back to the hotel."

As she felt the tears falling, she silently gasped. She realized that she wasn't alone. With her head still bowed, through blurry eyes, she saw two pair of dark, shiny shoes and dark suit pants. Her heart pounded with terror. The Mafia!

7

New Friends

"Can we help you?" AJ heard a kind voice speaking to her.

She looked up into the faces of two young men. They were wearing dark suits; and on their lapels were badges which read, "The Church of Jesus Christ of Latter-day Saints."

"Missionaries!" AJ blurted. "You're missionaries from the Church." AJ's heart skipped a beat. *Oh, thank you, thank you, Heavenly Father,* she kept saying over and over in her mind.

"This is Elder Borg," said one of the missionaries. "And I am Elder Stevens. How did you know we were missionaries?"

AJ could hardly gather her composure. She wanted to hug them and shout for joy. "I'm a Mormon," AJ answered. "The minute I saw your badges, I knew you were missionaries. You really are an answer to my prayers," she continued. "The reason I was standing there with my head bowed was because I was praying for help. At first, when I saw your shoes and dark suits, I thought you might be the Mafia or someone else who wanted to kidnap me."

The elders laughed. "We've never been compared to Mafia men or kidnappers before," Elder Borg said.

AJ looked up at the two young men, who were still laughing. *I must sound pretty dumb,* she thought. *But they will never know how thankful I am to have them here. I've never been so scared in my whole life.*

"How come you need help?" asked Elder Stevens. "Are you lost?"

"Yes, I am," replied AJ. "I can't find my way back to my hotel. I came here with a friend, but his grandmother became ill, and he left with her in the ambulance. At first I thought I could find my way back, but somehow I started walking in circles."

"Where's your hotel?" asked Elder Borg.

"It's by Faneuil Hall," AJ replied. "Do you know where that is?"

"We sure do," said Elder Stevens. "Let's start walking, and you can tell us the whole story on the way."

As they walked quickly towards Faneuil Hall, AJ told the missionaries about Tim and how she wanted to give a Book of Mormon to his grandmother. She told them how they went to meet his grandmother, who had become seriously ill. She explained how she had tried to find Paul Revere's house after Tim left with the ambulance. She also told them about Grelda and Taffy.

"My dad's probably out of his business meeting by now and looking for me," AJ continued. "That's why I need to hurry back."

The missionaries listened attentively to AJ's story.

"Elder Borg and I were out tracting about three blocks from where you were, AJ," said Elder Stevens. "We had just bought ourselves a pretzel when Elder Borg said he had a strong feeling that we were needed by someone. But the pretzels were especially good, and we tried to ignore his impression. Then Elder Borg said he couldn't stand it any longer. The thought kept coming to him, only stronger."

Elder Borg interrupted. "Really, AJ, the feeling was so strong within me. We started walking in your direction, not knowing why. But when we saw you huddled against the brick wall, we both looked at each other and knew instantly that you were the reason I had had those feelings."

AJ tingled inside. How thankful she was they had listened to those promptings. If they hadn't, she could still be back there waiting for help.

At last AJ spotted Faneuil Hall in the distance. Her heart was pounding. She was excited to get back and she was anxious to see her father.

As they rushed through the lobby doors, AJ saw her dad with Mary, both looking terrified.

"Dad! Dad!" AJ called. She ran into his arms.

"Where on earth have you been?" he asked. "Mary and I have been looking all over for you. We were about to call the police for help."

Mary grabbed AJ and hugged her. "I'm so glad you're okay. I've been worried about you. Didn't Tim bring you back? He promised me he would."

"I have so much to tell you," said AJ. "But first, I want you to meet Elder Borg and Elder Stevens. They rescued me, Dad. You'll never believe how they found me."

Her father shook hands with the elders, and Mary again hugged AJ. "Why don't we all go into the lobby and sit down while AJ tells us what happened," said Mary. "I just need to sign out at the desk."

They listened attentively as AJ explained in detail the happenings of the afternoon. As she finished telling how the elders had found her, she had a look of deep concern.

"I don't know what happened to Tim's grandmother," AJ said. "I don't know if she's even alive. Is there any way we can find out?"

"I know where Grandmother Hancey lives," said Mary. "Maybe if we call the hospitals in the vicinity, we can find her."

Mary went over to the desk and scanned the phone book. After making a few calls, she came back with a grin. "I found the hospital. But they wouldn't give out any information on Mrs. Hancey. Should we all go and see how she's doing?"

Both Elder Borg and Elder Stevens said they had no appointments that evening, and AJ's father was all through with his business meetings. Mary was as anxious as AJ to see how Grandmother Hancey was doing. So they all left for the hospital. Since it was quite a distance away, Mary suggested they take the MBTA.

AJ was fascinated as they went down several stairs. It seemed to her like going into a huge, cement basement. They got tickets and then boarded the underground train.

"I'm sure glad you know where we're going," Dad said to Mary. He looked over at AJ. "At least we won't get lost."

At last AJ could laugh about her afternoon scare.

The train zoomed through the tunnels. At intervals it came to an abrupt stop; then, just as suddenly, it started again. At each stop, the train doors opened automatically, and passengers scrambled to get on or get off.

"Here we are," Mary said at one stop, and she motioned for them to depart.

AJ quickened her step to keep up with everyone. Finally they were out of the tunnel and in the open again, but it was getting a little chilly, since the sun was almost down. AJ wished she had her jacket with her.

"I think the hospital is in this direction," Mary said.

Everyone walked even faster. It seemed they sensed an urgency. At least, AJ was able to keep warm by walking so fast.

As they entered the Boston hospital, Mary quickly found the front desk, where she asked for information about Adelaide Hancey.

"She's in Intensive Care right now," Mary said when she rejoined the group. "They're trying to find a doctor who can give us some information."

AJ looked in the direction of a sitting room. She grabbed her dad's arm. "I think that's Tim over there, Dad. Let's go see."

While Mary and the missionaries waited for a

doctor, AJ and her father walked over to where Tim was sitting. AJ noticed he no longer looked arrogant, as if he knew everything. He was slumped down in the chair, staring at the wall.

"Tim," AJ said quietly, "I'd like you to meet my dad, Mr. Bexton."

Tim swung around and at first he almost scowled, until he realized it was AJ.

"Hello, Tim," said AJ's father. "AJ told us about your grandmother, and we're here to see if we can do anything."

Tim stood up. "How did you know where to find me?" he asked.

AJ explained how Mary had called the different hospitals in the area.

"What was wrong with your grandmother?" asked AJ.

"Grandma has had a bad heart attack," replied Tim. "She's still in Intensive Care, and the doctors said they don't know if she'll make it or not."

Tim's voice was shaky, and AJ couldn't help but feel sorry for him. Then she had an idea.

"Tim, I don't know if you'll go for this or not, but at least you can hear my idea," said AJ. "My father and the missionaries could give Grandmother a blessing."

Tim looked over at AJ. "What do you mean by that?" he asked. "I don't think they'll even let anyone near her."

"AJ's talking about a priesthood blessing, Tim," explained AJ's father. "In our church, those who have authority can bless the sick. If you would like us to administer to your grandmother, I can check

53

with the two missionaries and see if either one of them has oil with them. When we bless the sick, we use a few drops of consecrated oil which is put on the head of the one being blessed. Then we ask our Father in Heaven to bless that person."

Tim looked puzzled.

"Tim, I know this might sound strange to you. And I know how you feel about religion," said AJ. "But I also know you love your grandmother. And I know you don't want her to die. I've seen Dad bless a sick person. I know there's a power there that is very real. If people have faith, and if Heavenly Father wants it to be, the sick can be made well."

"What do you mean, if people have faith?" Tim scoffed. "You know I don't have any faith in your religion. You know how I feel. I don't need any help from someone I can't see or from someone who has never helped me before." Tim was almost angry.

"Maybe you don't believe, Tim, but I do," said AJ. "And I have faith that Heavenly Father will hear our prayers."

Tim sat down. "I don't know," he murmured.

AJ sat down beside him. "I know you feel that your prayers weren't answered when your parents died. But maybe they were—only in a way you didn't understand. Think of the love you have for your grandmother. Think of all the good times you two have had together. Even though you believe that you were left alone at a time when you needed help, maybe you weren't. Maybe Heavenly Father has been watching over you all this time, and maybe it's time you prayed to him again."

Mary rushed over to the gathering. The mission-

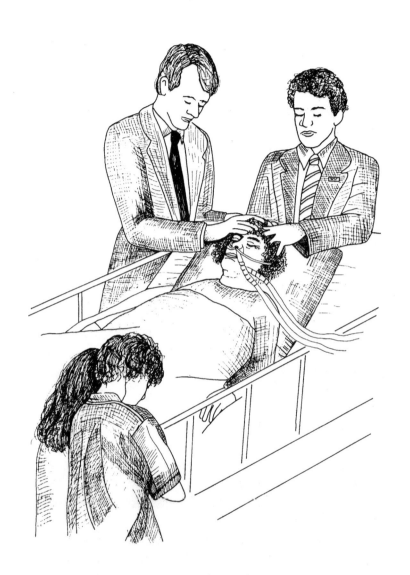

aries were at her side. AJ knew something was wrong. Tears were in Mary's eyes.

"Tim, you've got to come quick," she blurted. "The doctors say that Grandmother is losing ground fast. She might not live much longer."

"What do we do?" Tim cried. "Please, Mr. Bexton, can you help Grandma?"

"Elder Borg, do you have some oil with you?" AJ's father asked.

Both elders held up key chains, each with a vial of oil attached.

"Let's get the doctor," he said.

They were quickly ushered into a small room where Grandmother was hooked up to several tubes. She looked terribly pale.

AJ noticed that the minute her father started blessing Grandmother, Tim bowed his head. She could tell he was crying. AJ hurt for him. *Please answer our prayers, Heavenly Father,* she pleaded silently. *Please bless Grandmother Hancey. Please bless Tim.*

When the blessing was over, the doctors asked everyone but Tim to leave. As AJ was leaving the room, she saw him standing over his grandmother, reaching for her hand. It was almost more than AJ could bear to watch.

Out in the foyer of the hospital, Mr. Bexton and the missionaries talked quietly. Mary walked over and put her arm around AJ.

"That was a wonderful blessing your father gave to Tim's grandmother," Mary said. "It really touched Tim. I noticed he had tears in his eyes. From what his grandmother told me about him, Tim didn't seem like the kind of kid who would ever cry."

"I think you're right, Mary," AJ agreed. "I just hope our prayers are answered. I don't know what Tim would do without his grandmother. He'd be all alone."

"I'm sure Tim has thought about that," said Mary. "That's probably the only reason he consented to her having the blessing."

Tim walked out into the foyer.

"How's your grandmother doing?" asked AJ's father.

"She's resting right now," replied Tim. "The doctor said it will depend on how she does during the next five or six hours."

"You look so tired and you must be hungry, Tim," said Mary. "C'mon, AJ. You and I will run across the street to a deli and pick up some sandwiches. I've also got to find a phone and call my sister. She'll be worried if I don't come home."

"Is that okay, Dad?" AJ asked her father.

"Sounds like a great idea," he said. "I think all of us could use something to eat." He reached into his pocket and handed AJ some money. "Why don't you pick us up some of those Boston pretzels, too."

"I guess we'd better be on our way," said Elder Stevens.

"I was hoping you'd stay and have dinner here with us," said AJ's father. "Do you have some meetings scheduled?"

"Not exactly," said Elder Borg. "But we don't want to get in the way."

"Please stay," said AJ. "Dad gave me enough money to buy sandwiches and pretzels for everyone."

"And besides," said Mr. Bexton, "I think Tim would like to ask you two missionaries some questions. Am I right?" he asked, turning to look at Tim.

Tim nodded in agreement. There were a lot of questions he needed to have answered. "Here, AJ, take my sweater," he said turning to his new friend. "It's pretty cold outside."

"Thanks," said AJ. She grinned at him. "We'll be back before long."

8

Grelda

AJ and Mary rushed to the deli.

"Oh, no," moaned Mary, when they got close enough to see it. "The deli is closed for remodeling. C'mon, we'll go up the street a couple of blocks to another little sandwich shop." She headed off briskly, and AJ caught up.

"I hope they have pretzels covered with cheese," said AJ. "You were right when you told me how good they are. I love them."

Mary laughed. "They're my downfall, AJ. I could eat them every day."

"I can understand why you'd like to move out here," said AJ. "I've been here only one day and I love this city."

"Except when you're lost, right?" teased Mary.

AJ laughed. That all seemed so long ago. So much had happened in the last couple of hours.

"How long are you going to stay in Boston?" asked AJ.

"My sister's going to have a baby soon. So, probably after the baby is born, I'll go back to Utah," said Mary. "I've already gone to BYU for two years and I want to go back and get my degree."

"What are you studying?" asked AJ.

"I want to be a nurse," said Mary. "I love that kind of stuff—I mean, helping people, and things like that."

"What do you want to be when you grow up, AJ?" Mary asked.

"You'll probably laugh. But I really want to be a writer someday," replied AJ. "I love to write stories about people I know and about places I've been. But there's also something else I want to do."

"What's that?" asked Mary.

AJ was glad it was dark. She felt her cheeks flushing a little. "I really want to go on a mission when I'm older. Lots of girls do, you know. Does that sound funny?"

"Heavens, no," said Mary. "I've thought about that, too. In fact, I have thought a lot about it. Tell me again where your brother is serving."

"He's serving in Germany," said AJ. "He writes and tells me about some of the people he's teaching. I get so excited when I read his letters. I sometimes dream about being over there with him. I just don't think there'd be anything quite as exciting as telling people about the Church."

"I know what you mean," said Mary. "Missionaries are special people. And they seem to be guided a lot by Heavenly Father—just as Elder Borg and Elder Stevens were, when they found you."

AJ took hold of Mary's hand. She was so glad

she'd met Mary. They seemed to understand each other, even though Mary was older.

"Here's the deli," Mary said. "Let's hurry and order some sandwiches, so we can get back to the hospital before they start worrying about where we are."

As they waited for the sandwiches to be made, AJ stepped over by the window. She noticed a gathering of people and wondered what was going on. Off in the distance she heard a siren, and suddenly her heart pounded. She had heard the same siren when the ambulance came for Grandmother Hancey, and now the memories of the afternoon flooded her mind.

"What's going on out there?" asked Mary. "It sounds like an accident or something."

"I think someone's hurt," said AJ. "There's an ambulance and police."

"Here are our sandwiches, AJ," called Mary.

AJ left the window and returned to the deli counter to pay for the food. But her thoughts were on the crowd outside.

As she and Mary walked into the chilly outdoors, AJ grabbed Mary's arm.

"Let's go see what's going on," AJ said. "It'll just take a minute." For some reason, AJ felt very nervous. She just had to know what was happening.

Mary and AJ squeezed through the crowd. Two paramedics, just like the ones who'd helped Grandmother Hancey, were bending over somebody.

"It's just an old beggar woman," said a bystander. "She must have passed out from all of her booze."

The crowd started dispersing. Just an old beggar woman.

"I guess we might as well go, ourselves," said Mary. "There's probably nothing we can do to help."

She and AJ turned to go. But suddenly AJ jerked around. She had seen that old dress somewhere before.

"Grelda!" she exclaimed. "Mary, that old woman is Grelda!"

"AJ, get hold of yourself," said Mary, holding AJ back.

"Mary, I know that old lady," said AJ. "I've got to help her."

AJ rushed toward the scene and, before the paramedics could lift the body into the ambulance, AJ looked into the woman's weathered face. It *was* Grelda! Her eyes were closed, and AJ couldn't tell whether she was breathing.

"Grelda," AJ whispered into the old woman's ear. "Grelda. This is your little girl."

Slowly the old woman's eyes opened slightly, and a smile crossed her face. "Hello, my little girl," the old woman faintly whispered back.

Before AJ could say anything the paramedics pushed the stretcher into the ambulance.

"She's just an old bag lady, little girl," said one of the paramedics. "Looks like she's had a bad fall, and we're going to take her to the hospital."

"She's not just an old lady," AJ sobbed. "She's my friend."

Mary was at AJ's side. "Where are you taking her?" Mary asked. "Just let us know, so we can check on her, okay?"

"We're going to the hospital that's a few blocks

from here," answered the paramedic. And with that, he jumped into the ambulance and it sped away.

"How do you know her?" asked Mary, as she handed AJ some tissue to wipe her tears.

"I met her when I was lost," said AJ. "She said I could have lunch with her. And then she went to the garbage, and that's where she got her lunch. She kept talking to me, but I didn't think she'd ever remember who I was because she seemed to be thinking of other things. She had this old dog. Its name was Taffy."

AJ turned around. "Mary, let's see if he's around here somewhere."

"Here, Taffy. C'mere, Taffy," AJ called.

From out of the alley, the old, mangy, yellow dog appeared.

"Taffy!" AJ shouted. "See, Mary. I told you she had an old yellow dog."

AJ ran over to the dirty animal. "I've got to find some help for you, too," she said. "Mary, where can we put him?"

Mary was stunned. First the old lady. Now this old dog.

"Let's just give him one of these sandwiches," Mary suggested. "He'll probably stay around here pretty close, waiting for more food. Maybe we can figure out something to do with him later. First, we'd better get back to the hospital."

AJ and Mary ran toward the hospital. No longer did AJ notice how cold it was. She had to find Grelda.

When AJ and Mary rushed into the foyer, AJ's father and the missionaries were sitting across from

Tim. Elder Borg was holding a flip-chart. AJ and Mary stopped abruptly, not wanting to interrupt the peaceful scene. The missionaries were actually teaching Tim the gospel, right there, in the hospital. AJ thought that was one of the neatest things she'd ever seen.

"Why are you two all out of breath?" asked AJ's father. "I hope you remembered to bring us some dinner. We're starved."

"Dad, you'll never believe what happened," AJ said. "When Mary and I went to buy some sandwiches, we saw an ambulance pick up someone. It was an old lady I met today. Her name is Grelda. They were going to bring her to this hospital. Can we find out where she is?"

"Just let me grab a sandwich," said her dad. "The lady at the desk will know who was brought in the emergency entrance." Leaving the rest of the sandwiches with Mary and the young men, AJ and her father headed for the front desk.

"Yes, we did have someone brought in just a few minutes ago," said the nurse. "She's in the Emergency Room right now. If you want to go down, just follow the left corridor and it will lead you to Emergency."

"Thanks," said AJ as she and her father started walking.

"Wait for me," called Mary.

"We'd better come, too," said both missionaries, grabbing their sandwiches. "C'mon, Tim," they urged.

Soon the Emergency Room lobby was filled with people eager to know how Grelda was.

When the doctor walked into the foyer, he was surrounded. "Are all of you here wondering about the old lady who was just brought in?" he asked incredulously. "I thought she was just some old bag lady with no family."

"We're her friends," said AJ. "Is she going to be all right?"

The doctor smiled. "She took a pretty bad fall and scraped her legs up. I think her eyesight must be a little dim, so she couldn't see the curb. She hasn't any broken bones, but she's pretty weak. It looks like she's not had too much to eat the last several days."

AJ recalled Grelda eating the last of someone's sandwich which she had found in the garbage. That must have been all she'd had to eat.

"How long are you going to keep her?" asked AJ's father.

"Probably just a couple of days, so we can help her build up her strength a little," replied the doctor. "It's too bad we don't have better ways to take care of our older people who don't have anyone to care for them," he added.

"Can we go see her?" asked AJ.

"Yes," said the doctor. "We've moved her into a ward with some other people. Just follow me."

AJ spotted Grelda in the bed over by the window. "Over here." She motioned for everyone to follow her.

Grelda's eyes were closed. But she looked so different, thought AJ. With a clean gown around her and the dirt wiped from her face, she didn't look at all frightening.

"Hello, Grelda," AJ whispered. "Here's your little girl."

AJ's father was surprised when he heard what AJ said.

"She called me her 'little girl,'" said AJ, looking up at her dad. "I don't think she ever did know my name."

Grelda's eyes slowly opened. "My little girl."

"Grelda," said AJ, "you are going to be just fine. The doctors will take good care of you. You'll get lots of good food to eat."

"Taffy. Taffy," Grelda moaned.

"Taffy's okay," said AJ, as she took hold of the old woman's hand. "We fed him a sandwich and we'll make sure he gets some food."

"Who on earth is Taffy?" asked Tim.

"Taffy's her dog," said AJ quietly.

Grelda's eyes slowly closed.

"I think we'd better leave for now," said AJ's father. "She needs some rest."

The procession slowly walked out of the emergency area and went back to the lobby. "I'm still starved," said AJ's father.

"Don't worry, Mr. Bexton," said Mary. "We've still got sandwiches and pretzels."

Everyone gathered around Mary for their late night dinner. Everyone was showing signs of being tired and worn out from the day's happenings.

"Why don't you come back to the hotel with us, Tim?" asked AJ's father. "We can get a cab and take Mary and the elders home. Then, we can catch some sleep and be here early in the morning."

Tim paused. He was really tired. "No, thanks," he finally said. "Grandmother's still critical. I couldn't sleep, anyway. I'll just stay here and sleep on one of these couches."

"Brother Bexton," said Elder Stevens, "would you mind coming with us to call our mission president. We'd like to stay with Tim, but we'll need his permission. He might want to talk with you."

"I think I'll sleep here, too," said Mary. "I told my sister I'd be here if she needed to call me."

"Dad," pleaded AJ, when her father returned, "can't we stay here, too? I want to be here when they tell Tim about his grandmother. I've never slept in a hospital. It looks like there's enough couches for all of us."

"Since I told the mission president I would stay with his missionaries, if you can stand an unshaven and unshowered father I think I'll stay, too," Mr. Bexton said. "Let's go ask the nurses if they have some extra blankets."

9

Boston

"AJ, it's time to wake up." Her father nudged her.

AJ rolled over and groaned. Her body felt twisted and stiff from sleeping on the couch. She rubbed her eyes to better focus them. Elder Borg and Elder Stevens were awake and stretching; and Tim was walking over to the nurse's desk. Mary was still asleep.

"What time is it, Dad?" AJ asked stretching her arms.

"It's about seven o'clock," he replied.

AJ noticed a doctor talking with Tim, so she and her father walked over to see what he was saying.

"Your grandmother slept well during the night," the doctor said. "I don't know what happened, but she made a remarkable recovery during the night. Her vital signs are nearly stable and she's breathing on her own. You'll probably be able to take her home Monday morning."

AJ grinned at her father. Her prayers had been answered.

Tim's shoulders relaxed. He looked so tired. He probably hadn't slept very much for worrying about Grandmother, thought AJ.

"Is she completely out of danger now?" AJ's father asked the doctor.

"As far as we can tell," he replied. "If you folks want to get cleaned up and have some breakfast, she'll be perfectly fine in our care."

"What about Grelda?" asked AJ.

The doctor looked confused.

"She's the old lady they brought in last night in Emergency. She'd fallen and scraped her legs badly," explained AJ.

The doctor's face sobered. "She had a rough night. She's terribly weak from malnutrition and I don't know if she's got the strength to pull herself out of this."

AJ's heart quickened. "Dad, can't we do something? The missionaries are still here. Could you give Grelda a blessing, too?"

AJ's father motioned for the missionaries. When they reached the desk, Mr. Bexton asked, "Would you elders be willing to give another blessing this morning? Grelda's not doing well at all. AJ would appreciate it."

"Hey, that'd be great," said Elder Stevens. "Let's ask the doctor if it'd be okay."

AJ ran over and woke Mary. "Mary," she whispered. "Dad and the elders are going to give Grelda a blessing. We'll be back in just a few minutes."

"Wait for me," said Mary, with half-closed eyes. "I want to come, too."

"Me, too," chimed Tim.

Within minutes, Grelda's room was filled with her concerned friends.

"Grelda," whispered AJ, "this is my father and some missionaries from our church. They would like to give you a blessing to help you get better. Would that be okay?"

Grelda partially opened her eyes. She could barely manage a smile for AJ.

"Dad, Grelda's too weak to say anything," said AJ. "Please bless her to get well. And bless us to know what to do to help her."

AJ's father and the missionaries laid their hands on Grelda's head and gave a blessing of healing and comfort. A warm and peaceful feeling enveloped the hospital room.

"Let's let her rest, now," suggested AJ's father, after he'd given the blessing. "There's nothing more we can do. She's now in the Lord's hands."

AJ walked over and kissed Grelda lightly on her worn cheek. "I love you, Grelda," she whispered. "Be tough and try to live."

"Let's visit Grandmother," suggested Tim. "I'd like to see how she's doing."

Tim's grandmother was awake. "How are you feeling?" Tim asked, as his friends crowded into the room.

His grandmother smiled. It was apparent that she felt much better than the previous day. "I'm doing fine," she said. "They are even going to let me have breakfast this morning." She glanced around the room. "My, I sure have a lot of visitors for so early in the morning!"

"We're so glad you're doing okay," said Mary. "You gave us quite a scare."

Grandmother looked at the missionaries and at AJ's father. "I'm lucky that Tim and AJ brought her dad and these two fine young men. Are these the missionaries you've told me about?" she asked Mary.

"Yes, they are," answered Mary. She introduced them to Grandmother Hancey and then added, "I think they'd like to visit you when you get out of the hospital. Would that be okay?"

"What do you think, Tim?" his grandmother asked. "Do you think it'd be all right to have the elders come and tell us more about their church?"

Tim couldn't deny that he was interested. He shrugged his shoulders. "Sure, if that's what you'd like, Grandma," he answered.

A nurse entered the room. "Sorry," she told Grandmother's visitors. "Mrs. Hancey needs her breakfast and a bath. Could you come back later?" She ushered them out of the room after they all told Grandmother good-bye.

Out in the hospital foyer, AJ's father gathered them together. "Tim, your grandmother's doing well, and the doctor promised to keep a watchful eye on her. Why don't all of us go back to my hotel room and clean up and then go to breakfast? It'd do us all good to have a warm meal."

Everyone agreed. Mary called her sister to explain the situation. The missionaries' apartment was close to Faneuil Hall. They wanted to go there to shower and change clothes. Everyone decided to meet at Faneuil Hall at nine o'clock, sharp. AJ's father promised to treat them to a great breakfast.

"Do you really think the blessing your father gave Grandmother was what helped her?" Tim asked AJ, as they rode in the back seat of the taxi to the hotel.

AJ smiled at Tim. "I know it helped. Couldn't you feel something inside when Dad blessed her?"

"Yeah," said Tim, "I could feel something, but I don't know how to really explain it."

"I once heard that when you get a warm, peaceful feeling inside and it feels good, then you know that what you're witnessing is true," said AJ.

The taxi turned into the hotel parking lot.

"As soon as we've finished our breakfast," said AJ's father, "we'll go see some of the sights of Boston. I don't have any more meetings to attend. How does that sound?"

"That'll be fun," said Mary. "I'm so glad I don't have to work today."

Before leaving the hotel, AJ's father made a quick call to the hospital, just to make sure Grandmother and Grelda were okay. Grandmother was recuperating fine. Grelda was still critical, but improving; and the doctors felt she'd pull through just fine. Both Tim and AJ relaxed at the good news.

When everyone met at Faneuil Hall, they quickly agreed to eat breakfast there, out in the fresh air, under an umbrella.

"Let's walk to the Boston Common and begin our sightseeing there," suggested AJ's father. "We can stop and make periodic calls to the hospital. Is that okay with everyone?"

Except for the missionaries, who had appointments that morning, the group agreed. After a hearty breakfast the elders left and the four sight-seers found the red brick trail and followed it to the Common.

"This is really a lot different than I thought it'd be," said AJ. "It looks like a huge park."

Trees adorned the lavish green lawns. The gleaming gold-domed State House was a magnificent sight on the hill overlooking the grounds. As they walked along, they saw bronze monuments depicting moments and people from the past.

"AJ," called Tim, motioning, "you'll really like this."

They walked into a graveyard.

"This is kinda eerie," said AJ. "It looks like someplace where you'd film a spooky movie."

The trees had long, spindly, gnarled branches which hung low. Some even draped over the black wrought-iron gate which surrounded the cemetery.

"Look," called Mary, "if you read the head-stones, you'll see that some of America's greatest patriots are buried here."

AJ was fascinated. She followed the narrow, dirt path around the many headstones. Some were cracked and broken. AJ was thrilled. Yet she still determined that this was not a place she'd like to visit on a dark, windy, rainy night.

They visited King's Chapel, the first Unitarian church in the country. But what caught AJ's attention was the Old Corner Bookstore on Washington and School Streets. She read a sign which said that some of New England's authors—Hawthorne, Emerson, and Thoreau and others—used to gather there.

She gazed in awe at the old, worn books. Every

niche seemed to be utilized in the compact store. She could have stayed for hours to just browse.

Close by, on Washington and Milk Streets, was Benjamin Franklin's birthplace. For some reason, AJ had thought he was born in Philadelphia. But he had been born in Boston and had lived there until he was seventeen. Then he left for Philadelphia.

By noontime, they were back at Faneuil Hall and Quincy Market.

"It's time for a phone call and a cheese-covered pretzel," announced AJ's father.

After they checked at the hospital and found everything was fine, they continued on the Freedom Trail.

They passed Paul Revere's brown frame house again. AJ remembered when she and Tim had gone inside. Not too far away was the Old North Church. They walked up the front steps to have a closer view. This was the old church where two lanterns were hung from the belfry to signal Paul Revere that the British were coming by sea.

"This is one of the first places my sister took me when I came to Boston," said Mary. "As she told me the story of the lights signaling Paul Revere, and how he rode through the towns calling, 'The British are coming, the British are coming,' I could almost imagine it happening."

"Girls are so funny," said Tim. "If you want to see something really interesting, let's go to the navy yard. It's not too far away. If the line isn't too long, we can even take a tour on 'Old Ironsides.' It's the oldest warship still in use in the world."

AJ's feet were getting tired from all the walking.

AJ & Tim   "The Old North Church"

But once the little touring group found the red line. of paint, they started again on their trek.

As they crossed over the harbor, Tim indicated where they were going.

"Are any of you guys getting tired from walking?" asked AJ's dad.

He heard moans and groans, and started laughing.

"Now you know how missionaries feel every night when they go to bed," he laughed.

"Benj rides a bike in Germany," said AJ. "I think I'd like that better."

"Here we are," said Tim. "There's hardly any line at all. Let's see how much the tickets are for a tour."

AJ's father went over to a small office. He came back waving tickets. "All aboard," he shouted.

The ship was much different than AJ had imagined. First of all, her father had to duck to keep from hitting his head on the ceiling. In fact, there were some places where even AJ had to duck.

"The sailors must have been really short," said AJ. "Or else they'd have to slump over to get around."

They saw the bunks where the sailors had slept. They saw the mess hall and even some of the tin plates and cups they had used. Nothing was fancy. The captain's quarters were nicer than the rest of the ship, but all the beds looked small and uncomfortable, even the captain's.

"What's this over here?" asked AJ, pointing to some rooms with iron grates.

"Those are probably for the sailors who are put into jail for doing something wrong," said Tim.

Life on the "Old Ironsides" would certainly be difficult, thought AJ. *And probably boring, too. I'd get pretty bored scrubbing these wooden floors and washing the tin plates and cups.*

As the group left the ship, it was already into the late afternoon.

"It's time for another phone call to the hospital," said AJ's father. "And then maybe we'd better start back in that direction. I think we've had enough history for one day."

"Does that mean we won't make it to Fenway Park?" asked AJ.

"Looks like it," answered her father. "That was something I really wanted you to see. I guess we'll have to come back someday."

"Come back when you can go to a game," suggested Tim. "That'd be a lot more fun than just going there to look at it."

AJ's father found a pay phone and called the hospital. A nurse told him that all was still well with both Grandmother Hancey and Grelda. Since it was close to dinner time, the sightseers decided to make their way to the intersection where they had arranged to meet the missionaries. The two elders had just arrived.

AJ had been so caught up in the sights of the day that she had nearly forgotten how worried she was about Grandmother and Grelda. But now that they were on their way to the hospital, once again questions loomed in her mind.

"Mary," she asked, "what are we going to do about Grelda? Once she's out of the hospital, she still has no one to care for her. And she'll probably just get sick again. At least Tim will be there to help Grandmother."

"I know," said Mary. "I've been thinking about her, too. I doubt if she has any family around."

Tomorrow was Sunday, and that was the day AJ would leave for Utah. *I just can't leave her all alone,* thought AJ. Suddenly AJ remembered Grelda's old, mangy dog. "Taffy," she murmured. "I wonder what happened to Taffy. I'd completely forgotten about him."

10

Decisions

"Let's go to that same deli where we got sandwiches last night," suggested AJ. She was hoping she might find Taffy still waiting around there for Grelda.

"Those *were* good sandwiches," said her father. "Okay. We'll stop there before we reach the hospital."

AJ stayed outside the deli and quietly called for Taffy while everyone else went inside to order. She was about to give up, when she saw a yellow, furry head peeking around the corner of the store.

"C'mere, Taffy," AJ called. The old mangy dog lumbered over to her.

Just then her father and the others came out of the deli. "AJ," he asked, "what are you doing with that dirty old dog?"

"Dad, meet Taffy," said AJ. "He's Grelda's dog. What can we do with him?"

"Ugh," scowled Tim. "He's so dirty and smelly. Why don't you just turn him over to the dog pound?"

"Tim Hancey!" declared AJ. "He just needs a bath."

"AJ," her dad interrupted, "Tim's got a point. He's really dirty and we don't have any way to clean him up. Besides, what would become of him, even if we did wash him? Who's going to feed him?"

Mary moved over by the yellow dog. "If we could clean him up, maybe I know of a place for him. My sister loves dogs and she's always helping out strays. It's worth a try. The main problem is that we don't have anyplace to wash him."

"We've got a big old tin tub at our apartment," said Elder Borg. "I always wondered what we'd use it for. If we can get Taffy to follow us home, we'll give him a bath."

"I know how you can get him to follow you," said AJ, excitedly. "Just take my sandwich and give him a little at a time till you get home. He'll follow."

She was right. One smell of the bread and the missionaries had a new friend.

"Should we all meet for church in the morning?" asked Elder Stevens. "We go to the building that's over in Cambridge. We can call you at the hotel and tell you how to get there. It's close to Longfellow's house."

"That'd be great!" said AJ's father.

"That's my church building, too," said Mary. "We must have different meeting schedules. I can tell the Bextons how to get there. What time do you meet?"

"At nine o'clock. Should we meet there about

8:45 tomorrow?" asked Elder Borg. "Then you can let us know how Tim's grandmother and Grelda are doing. And we can try to get Taffy all scrubbed clean."

"8:45 it is," said AJ's father. "We'll see you then. Here, take another sandwich for your dog."

AJ noticed that Tim hadn't said a word when they were talking about church. "Do you think you'd like to go with us, Tim?" she asked. "I mean, to church tomorrow morning?"

"I'd feel pretty dumb," said Tim. "I've not been to any church for so long, I can't even remember the last time."

"I think it'd make your grandmother really happy if you decided to go," said AJ. "Besides, I think the elders are planning to give you and your grandmother some lessons about the Church, if you want."

Tim shrugged his shoulders. He couldn't deny the feelings he'd had when he heard his grandmother being blessed. And he couldn't remember enjoying people quite as much as he had his new friends.

"Sure," he said. "I'll go with you. But I do want to stay with Grandmother tonight at the hospital. If it's okay, I'll just meet you at your hotel tomorrow morning at about eight o'clock."

AJ, her father, and Mary stayed at the hospital for a while, so they could visit with Grandmother. She felt good and was in a cheerful mood.

"I guess I'm going home on Monday," she announced. She looked at Tim. "I'm so lucky I've got you, Tim," she said, taking hold of his hand. "I don't know what I'd do without you."

AJ noticed Tim get a little teary. She knew that Tim didn't know what he'd do without his grandmother, and he'd come pretty close to finding out.

"Grandmother," said AJ, "Tim is going to church with us in the morning. Isn't that great?"

Grandmother's eyes lit with interest. "That's wonderful!" she exclaimed. "I wish I were going with you, too. There's a lot I want to learn about that church of yours. I hope Tim and I can have the chance."

AJ's father laughed. "I have a feeling that you'll be seeing a lot of Elder Borg and Elder Stevens. Right now, they're on their way home to scrub an old, yellow dog."

"I'll tell you all about that," said Tim. "Mr. Bexton and AJ are going to go back to the hotel. I'm staying here and will meet them in the morning."

Before leaving the hospital, AJ wanted to look in on Grelda, so they said good-bye to Tim and Grandmother and found their way to the other ward.

Grelda's eyes were closed, and AJ didn't know if she wanted to wake her. She tiptoed to her side and gently touched her hand. She was turning around to leave when she heard, "How's Grelda's little girl?"

AJ spun around. "Grelda," she said. "I'm glad you're awake. I have something so exciting to tell you. My friends are taking Taffy to their home tonight, so he'll be okay. Isn't that great?"

Grelda didn't say anything. Tears streamed down her cheeks. "Taffy is Grelda's dog. Please don't let anyone take him away."

"Oh, now," soothed AJ. "They're not taking him

away. They're just going to feed him and take care of him until you can."

Poor Grelda, thought AJ. *What is going to become of her? How can I fly back home, knowing she is here with no one to care for her?*

AJ hugged Grelda good-night and told her she'd see her tomorrow. "And for sure," AJ added, "Taffy is just fine and waiting for you."

"I called my sister," said Mary, as they walked out of Grelda's room. "She's on her way to pick us up. She said she'd be happy to take you back to your hotel."

AJ was tired and her feet ached from the day's walking. She was glad to get into a car and go to the hotel. She'd had so much fun seeing the sights of Boston, but it had worn her out. She was so thankful that Grandmother and Grelda were okay. The only part that bothered her was leaving Grelda behind.

After saying good-bye to Mary and her sister, AJ and her father entered the hotel.

"A hot bath sure will feel good tonight," said AJ. "My feet feel like I've walked a hundred miles."

"Mine, too," said her father. "I still need to read some documents tonight, so why don't we kneel and say prayers now. Then you can take a warm bath and crawl into your bed."

After her bath, AJ sat on her bed, holding pen and paper.

I think I'll write to Benj to tell him about my trip to Boston, AJ thought. *He'll never believe all that happened from giving away a copy of the Book of Mormon.*

She thought of her big brother in Germany, so far away. If he had a problem, what would he do? Of course, he'd pray about it. Why hadn't AJ thought to ask Heavenly Father about Grelda? Her father was in the other room, reading his business papers; so she quietly knelt by her bed. "Dear Heavenly Father," she began. "I have a real problem that I need help with."

11

Good-bye to Boston

AJ was up early, fixing her hair for church. "I'm so glad Tim's going to church with us," said AJ. "When I first told him about the Church, he laughed at me. But I think when he saw you give Grandmother a blessing he started to take it more seriously."

"Lots of times we don't pay attention until something comes along that's too big to handle alone," said her father. "Tim's a fine boy. I just hope there will be some boys his age at church who will befriend him. Then he'll feel more like coming."

AJ and her father walked into the hotel lobby. They looked around to see if Tim had arrived.

"Hi, AJ."

AJ immediately recognized Mary's friendly voice. She gave her a hug.

"Is Tim coming, for sure?" asked Mary. "He did seem a little hesitant."

"He'll come," said AJ.

But as the minutes ticked away, AJ thought maybe she was wrong.

"We've got to leave. We'll never make it on time if we wait any longer," said her father. "I'm sorry, AJ. I guess Tim changed his mind."

They walked outside the hotel. There were light clouds, yet it was quite warm. AJ's father hailed a taxi. They started to climb inside, when they heard someone calling, "AJ. Hey, wait up."

Tim rushed over. "Sorry about being late. It took me longer to get here than I planned." He jumped into the taxi beside AJ.

What a great day this is, thought AJ. She was grateful that Tim had really come.

Standing in front of the church doors were Elder Borg and Elder Stevens. "You'll never believe the time we had giving Taffy a bath last night," Elder Borg said. "*We* were soaked, by the time we finally rinsed the soap off *him*."

"But you've got to see him. He's actually a good-looking dog," added Elder Stevens.

"We'd better go inside," said AJ's father.

"We have sacrament meeting first," said Elder Stevens, "so just go into the chapel."

The church was different than AJ's building back home. It didn't look too much like a church. In fact, it looked more like a big white house. But there was a good feeling inside. And she was so glad to be there.

"After the meeting, we can walk over to Longfellow's home," said Mary. "You'll love it, AJ. It looks just like it did when he lived there."

AJ watched as her father showed Tim where to sit. The missionaries sat down next to him. How she hoped that Tim's heart would be touched by the meeting, so he'd want to learn more about the Church!

AJ whispered to Elder Borg, "There aren't very many little kids in this ward. And there's hardly anyone my age."

"Most of the members are students who are going to Harvard or MIT," he replied. "We do have quite a few babies. You'll hear them during testimony meeting."

AJ had forgotten that it was the first Sunday of the month. She always did enjoy hearing people share their testimonies. Maybe Tim would also.

After the sacrament, a member of the bishopric stood at the pulpit. As he shared his testimony of the gospel, AJ's thoughts filtered back to the happenings of the last two days. She recalled giving Grandmother the Book of Mormon. It was probably still in the corner of the big chair that Grandmother had been sitting in when she became ill.

She recalled being lost. She had a lot to be thankful for. Suddenly, she felt a burning inside her. Her heart started to pound, and she felt she should share some of her feelings. She arose and walked up to the pulpit as soon as the counselor sat down.

Her voice was shaky, and she felt her stomach churning with anxiety. She looked at Tim, the missionaries, Mary, and her father. She thought of Grandmother and Grelda.

"Dear Brothers and Sisters," she began, "my name is AJ Bexton and I'm from Utah. I came here with my father for the weekend. While he was at a business meeting, I met some very special people. I think Heavenly Father meant for me to come to Boston.

"You see, I promised my big brother Benj, who is on a mission in Germany, that I would give away a Book of Mormon to someone in Boston. I met Mary, who is from Utah, too. She's great. Then I met another friend, Tim Hancey. I want to thank him for showing me the sights of Boston. I love this city. I love his grandmother. I'm glad Tim's my friend. I hope he always remembers these last two days and some of the things we've been through. I hope he will someday read the book I gave to his grandmother.

"Then I met two more special people. They are here in this meeting: Elder Borg and Elder Stevens. At first I thought they were Mafia men."

Some of the people in the congregation couldn't help but chuckle. And AJ saw the elders' faces flushing.

"I'm so thankful they listened to the promptings they felt. I also met another person. She also lives in your city. But none of you know her. She's a bag lady. I met her when she was finding lunch out of the garbage. She's a wonderful person who needs food and someone to care about her. The only one she has is an old yellow dog. The missionaries gave him a bath so we could all stand to have him around. He smelled pretty bad. I'm going back to Utah this afternoon and I need to know if someone will help me help her."

Tears filled AJ's eyes. Every person in the audience was listening attentively to her words.

"When I get home, I'm going to ask people in my ward to help Grelda. My Merrie Miss class can do projects to help raise money for her. The Relief Society can gather things to send her. But is there anyone in the audience who has one room where she can sleep?"

AJ could hardly contain her emotions. But she finally added, "I've asked Heavenly Father to help Grelda. But the only answer I keep receiving is that he helps us through other people. He can't give Grelda food or a place to sleep unless we help him help her.

"I thank Heavenly Father for all the times he's answered my prayers. I know he loves us all.

"I say this in the name of Jesus Christ. Amen."

A hushed "amen" echoed throughout the chapel.

A gentleman walked to the pulpit. Wiping his eyes, he began, "Young lady from Utah, I know you."

AJ looked up. Sure enough, it was the old gentleman who had nearly sat on her at the airport when she was waiting for her dad to go home and get her backpack. He smiled at her.

"I knew there was something special about you when I met you in the airport," he said. "But I had no idea that I'd ever see you again. You've just touched my stingy old heart, and I think it's high time I let the Lord know I'm grateful for his goodness to me. I've got a room in my home where the grandkids stay when they come. But they don't come very often. It's not much. But it's warm. And sometimes on a cold, winter night, it'd be mighty nice for my wife and me to have some company. I also have a fence around my little backyard. Maybe that old yellow dog would like a place to stay, too. So, after this meeting, you come and see me. We'll set up a way for your friend to come to my home. That's on one condition—you've got to promise that someday you'll come back to Boston and visit us."

If it hadn't been a sacrament meeting, everyone in the audience would probably have stood and clapped. Some people were wiping their eyes, and others were smiling at each other and whispering that this was the greatest meeting they'd ever attended.

AJ's father was crying. Mary was crying. The missionaries were crying. Tim grinned at AJ and held up two thumbs.

"You Mormons are all right," Tim whispered. "After I've read the book you gave Grandmother, I'll write and let you know what I think about it."